It Was The Night Before Christmas
(Let's Not Forget)

Jason Holloway

ISBN 978-1-0980-8911-5 (hardcover)
ISBN 978-1-0980-8912-2 (digital)

Copyright © 2022 by Jason Holloway

All rights reserved. No part of this publication may be reproduced, distributed, or transmitted in any form or by any means, including photocopying, recording, or other electronic or mechanical methods without the prior written permission of the publisher. For permission requests, solicit the publisher via the address below.

Christian Faith Publishing, Inc.
832 Park Avenue
Meadville, PA 16335
www.christianfaithpublishing.com

Printed in the United States of America

This book is dedicated to those with wondering eyes, Christmas cheer, and to everyone trying to make room in the inn.

Merry Christmas

It was the night before Christmas, but all through the town,
For Joseph and Mary, no room could be found.

Tired and weary from their journey's demands,
They found shelter in a stable with cattle and lambs.

While children were nestled all snug in their beds,
Mary and Joseph had a long night ahead.
The prophets foretold, now the time was at hand,
For the birth of a Savior in ol' Bethlehem.

I wonder if Mary watched in dismay,
As they pulled out a manger and filled it with hay.
An angel had told her this child would be king,
Birth in a stable was not what she dreamed.

The stars in the heavens burned brightly that night,
But the brightest of all shone down on this sight.
And men in a country known to be wise,
Had seen the great star and guessed at its sign.

They loaded their bags with frankincense and gold,
To search for this child, God's gift to the world.
They left on their journey with this thought in mind:
Away in a manger lay the greatest gift of all time.

Then shepherds who watched over their flocks that night,
Heard heavenly carols being sung from on high.
When what to their wondering eyes should appear?
A glorious angel with news of good cheer.

"Fear not," he said. "There's no reason to mourn.
For unto you this day, a Savior is born.
The Lord of all creatures wears not kingly robes,
But rests in a manger wrapped in swaddling clothes."

Christmas these days is full of trees, gifts, and lights.
Santa will come down the chimney tonight.
He will leave lots of toys, presents, and cheer,
Then fly off in his sleigh, 'til Christmas next year.

And while each year ol' Santa, I love to see,
There is another in whom I believe.

A baby whose birth brought joy to the world,
The gift of salvation to all boys and girls.
He came to the Earth so humble and meek,
With no room in the inn that first Christmas Eve.

He is the Reason, the Hope, and the Light.
So let's not forget that first Christmas night.

About the Author

Jason Holloway lives his life guided by faith in Jesus Christ and a belief in Santa Claus. As a top-secret Santa operative, he oversees and executes confidential Christmas missions each year. While the details of these missions remain classified, they reportedly involve stockings, presents, and Christmas cheer. More importantly, Holloway strives to stand as a witness of God and live as a disciple of Jesus Christ. He resides in the great state of Texas with his wife, four children, and a basset hound named Betty White.

CPSIA information can be obtained
at www.ICGtesting.com
Printed in the USA
BVHW011111141222
654208BV00007B/587